For Our
Wonderful
New Members

For Our
Wonderful
New Members

DAISAKU IKEDA

World Tribune
Press

Published by World Tribune Press

A division of the SGI-USA
606 Wilshire Blvd.
Santa Monica, CA 90401

Cover and interior design by Lightbourne, Inc.
Credits for images: iStockPhoto: pp. i, vi, 4, 16, 32, 64,
    Seikyo Press: p. 49, Shutterstock: pp. iii, 48.

24 23 22 21 20   1 2 3 4 5

ISBN: 978-1-944604-33-2

Library of Congress Control Number: 2019913926

CONTENTS

EDITOR'S NOTE

*F*OR OUR WONDERFUL NEW MEMBERS IS A collection of five essays by SGI President Ikeda in his series titled "The Buddhism of the Sun—Illuminating the World." They were first published in *Living Buddhism* from May to September 2019.

The citations most commonly used in this book have been abbreviated as follows:

> **LSOC,** page number(s) refers to *The Lotus Sutra and Its Opening and Closing Sutras*, translated by Burton Watson (Tokyo: Soka Gakkai, 2009).

> **OTT,** page number(s) refers to *The Record of the Orally Transmitted Teachings*, translated by Burton Watson (Tokyo: Soka Gakkai, 2004).

> **WND,** page number(s) refers to *The Writings of Nichiren Daishonin*, vol. 1 (WND-1) (Tokyo: Soka Gakkai, 1999) and vol. 2 (WND-2) (Tokyo: Soka Gakkai, 2006).

ONE

A Teaching of Mentor and Disciple—Let's Walk the Path to Happiness Together

N ICHIREN BUDDHISM IS THE SUPREME WAY to develop wisdom to achieve happiness and peace. It is a teaching that enriches each person's life while striving to elevate the life state of humanity and create a society in which people can live in harmony.

The Soka Gakkai is growing dynamically as a global religious movement of the twenty-first century. All of you, our new members who have joined us at this time have a mission imbued with "great good fortune from past existences" (LSOC, 356), just as Buddhism teaches.

Here, together with our treasured new members whom I love and respect, and with friends who have been studying Buddhism up till now, I would like to discuss the core principles and practice of Nichiren Buddhism. I intend to write as if we were seated together in a shady grove cooled by gentle breezes, engaging in a relaxed conversation. First, we will

1

study about mentor and disciple, the core spirit of Buddhism, the most basic principle of a humanistic philosophy.

Communicating the Spirit and Actions of My Mentor

My mentor is Josei Toda, the second Soka Gakkai president. I would not be the person I am today were it not for him. My two novels, *The Human Revolution* and *The New Human Revolution,* which I have spent the better part of my life writing, are nothing other than the fulfillment of a promise I made to him deep in my heart.

In 1957, I resolved: "It is my mission to leave a record of Mr. Toda's life for the sake of posterity!" On August 13 of that year, Mr. Toda called on me to join him in Karuizawa, Nagano Prefecture. At the time, I was engaged in an ongoing struggle against the devilish nature of authority, as the Soka Gakkai faced persecutions in the form of what's known as the Yubari Coal Miners Union Incident[1] and the Osaka Incident.[2]

In one of my conversations with my mentor in Karuizawa, the subject came up of his newly published novel, *Human Revolution.* The novel told the story of a man, modeled on Mr. Toda, striving to advance kosen-rufu together with his mentor, Tsunesaburo Makiguchi, the first Soka Gakkai president. It chronicled

kosen-rufu—A term from the Lotus Sutra that literally means to declare and spread widely. It refers to the process of securing lasting peace and happiness for all humankind by establishing the humanistic ideals of Nichiren Buddhism in society.

the true nature of the Soka Kyoiku Gakkai (Value-Creating Education Society), the precursor to the Soka Gakkai, and what it stood for.

Mr. Toda confessed with a smile, however, that while he had no trouble writing about Mr. Makiguchi, he found it too difficult to convey his own story fully. Those words struck me deeply.

Mr. Toda's novel concluded after describing his courageous struggle while imprisoned by the Japanese militarist authorities and his awakening to his mission as a Bodhisattva of the Earth [whom in the Lotus Sutra the Buddha entrusts with propagating the Mystic Law, the Lotus Sutra's essence]. He did not, however, record anything about his tremendous efforts to spread the teachings after his release.

Enabling a Change in the Destiny of All Humankind

The following day, August 14—the tenth anniversary of my first meeting with him—I vowed to write a sequel telling the true history of the Soka Gakkai spirit in Mr. Toda's place.

Seven years later, in Okinawa on December 2, 1964, I began writing *The Human Revolution*, the story of Mr. Toda's life dedicated to kosen-rufu. Its central theme is "A great human revolution in just a single individual will help achieve a change in the destiny of a nation and, further, will enable a change in the destiny of all humankind."[3] And for the past twenty-five years, I have been writing *The New*

Human Revolution, describing the endeavors of his disciples to make their mentor's vision a reality. Now, that literary journey of the shared struggle of mentor and disciple has been completed, and I have been able to fulfill my vow to my mentor.[4]

The Wish to Help All People to Become Buddhas

It must be ties of karma from the distant past that have destined you to become my disciple at a time like this. Shakyamuni and Many Treasures[5] certainly realized this truth. The [Lotus Sutra's] statement, "Those persons who had heard the Law dwelled here and there in various Buddha lands, constantly reborn in company with their teachers," cannot be false in any way. (WND-1, 217)

This passage from Nichiren's "The Heritage of the Ultimate Law of Life" teaches the deep karmic ties that link mentor and disciple as expounded in Buddhism. To receive the "heritage of the ultimate Law of life" mentioned in the title means, very simply, to inherit the most important teaching for attaining Buddhahood, which is transmitted from the Buddha to ordinary people, from mentor to disciple.

In the Lotus Sutra's second chapter, "Expedient Means," the Buddha explains that he has aimed from the start "to make all persons equal to me, without any distinction between us" (LSOC, 70). Shakyamuni's true wish was to enable all people to attain the same life state of Buddhahood he had achieved.

Here, I would like to affirm that Buddhism is distinguished by its focus on human beings. A Buddha is an awakened human being—a person, just like the rest of us. The person first to awaken to the Law (the Buddha) teaches that Law, seeking to elevate the lives of all human beings. In that respect, the relationship between the Buddha and ordinary people is not like that between a god and human beings. Rather, it is a relationship between teacher and student, between mentor and disciple.

People of later ages lost sight of this core message, first by limiting the possibility of attaining enlightenment to people of a certain capacity who lived in a certain time. Second, they deified the Buddha, entirely separating him from human beings. The mentor-disciple relationship ceased to exist.

The Lotus Sutra [compiled centuries after the Buddha's death] corrects this distortion. It teaches the ultimate truth of Buddhism, that all people possess the supreme state of Buddhahood within them. And it describes the Buddha's efforts to enable all living beings to attain a life state equal to his own. The words "to make all persons equal to me, without any distinction between us" revive the humanistic essence of Buddhism.

Elevating the life state of disciples to the same level of the Buddha—this is the fundamental aim of Buddhism and the Lotus Sutra's most important theme. It is none other than the path of mentor and disciple, the oneness of mentor and disciple. Precisely because it grounds itself in the

> Elevating the life state of disciples to the same level of the Buddha—this is the fundamental aim of Buddhism and the Lotus Sutra's most important theme.

most noble spirit of mentor and disciple, through which the hearts of human beings connect, Nichiren Buddhism is a humanistic teaching, one in which ordinary people take the lead.

In "The Heritage of the Ultimate Law of Life," addressed to Sairen-bo,[6] Nichiren writes, "Nichiren has been trying to awaken all the people of Japan to faith in the Lotus Sutra so that they too can share the heritage and attain Buddhahood" (WND-1, 217). Nichiren vowed to transmit the heritage for attaining Buddhahood, which he had inherited from Shakyamuni through the Lotus Sutra, to all people in what's called the Latter Day of the Law, the impure age we are living in now. This passage elucidates the depth of the karmic ties linking Nichiren and his disciples.

It appears that the authorities persecuted Sairen-bo for embracing the Daishonin's teachings. Praising him for refusing to be defeated and remaining his disciple, the Daishonin says that he is "like pure gold" (WND-1, 217). He also writes, "It must be ties of karma from the distant past that have destined you to become my disciple at a time like this." The ties of mentor and disciple are not limited to this lifetime, the Daishonin asserts, but have existed since the distant past, countless lifetimes ago.

Joy in Both Life and Death

Answers to the questions of life and death are fundamentally what people seek from religion. As such, all of the world's religions, including Buddhism, teach something about the eternal. Life and death are fundamental concerns of religion. But the view of eternity differs from religion to religion. Buddhism teaches the continuity of life throughout the three existences—past, present, and future. Although it views the cycle of birth and death as perpetual, Buddhism does not emphasize an unending cycle of suffering, nor does it promote the desire to escape the difficult realities of life.

The Lotus Sutra expounds a view of life based on the eternal and fundamental Law of the universe. By chanting Nam-myoho-renge-kyo, our lives become characterized by supreme joy embodying the "four virtues": eternity, happiness, true self, and purity. That is, we attain a life state pervaded by joy in both life and death.

Central to the Lotus Sutra's view of life and death is that the bonds between mentor and disciple, who strive together to spread the Buddhist teachings, endure throughout past, present, and future. In "The Heritage of the Ultimate Law of Life," the Daishonin cites as evidence a passage from "The Parable of the Phantom City," the sutra's seventh chapter: "Those persons who had heard the Law dwelled here and there in various Buddha lands, constantly reborn in company with their teachers" (LSOC, 178).

Shakyamuni says here that his voice-hearer disciples (those "who had heard the Law")[7] had been his followers from the remote past, continually born with and carrying out bodhisattva practice alongside him in many different Buddha lands. On hearing Shakyamuni's preaching, they remember that innate within them exists the life state of the bodhisattva, dedicated to Buddhist practice with the wish to relieve the sufferings of all living beings. The role of their mentor, the Buddha, is to remind them of this profound wish.

This "profound wish" is the great vow for kosen-rufu. Bodhisattvas vow to carry out the wish of the Buddha, who has compassion and empathy for all people. That they have practiced the bodhisattva way with their mentor since the remote past indicates that the path to fundamentally relieving people's suffering goes on forever. Nichiren's assertion that this "cannot be false in any way" must have reinforced Sairen-bo's certainty of the deep ties of the mentor-disciple relationship in Buddhism.

My Unforgettable Encounter With Mr. Toda

I first met Mr. Toda on August 14, 1947, more than seven decades ago, at a discussion meeting in Tokyo's Ota Ward. Young as I was, he spoke to me warmly as if I were an old friend. Our conversation was the turning point that determined the rest of my life.

American scholar of religion Nicholas Gier said that three things impressed him about this encounter. First, though I was much younger than Mr. Toda, he treated me as an equal. Second, he spoke straightforwardly about the true nature of life, without difficult arguments or fancy words. Third, I, as a young man, was deeply moved that Mr. Toda had been arrested and imprisoned for opposing Japan's militarist government.[8] Dr. Gier went on to say that our encounter was a modern expression of the universal formula for humanism that defined Shakyamuni's interactions with his disciples, in which they personally developed by experiencing his great character and humanity.[9]

In fact, because Mr. Toda's character inspired me and I felt I could trust him implicitly, I joined the Soka Gakkai ten days later. I didn't know anything about Buddhism. I think many of you today studied the basics of Buddhism and learned about our movement from your friends in the Soka Gakkai before you joined. You had a much more structured and organized introduction to Buddhism than I did. At any rate, living my life with Mr. Toda and walking the path of mentor and disciple alongside him was the greatest honor of my youth.

In his copy of Nichiren's writings, Mr. Makiguchi underlined the passage "Entering into the relation of teacher and [disciple] is the result of a bond that bridges the three existences" (WND-2, 375). It is not by accident or coincidence that we have come to practice Nichiren Buddhism.

It is because of a profound karmic bond that persists throughout past, present, and future. And Mr. Makiguchi and Mr. Toda are the ones who led the way in teaching us the correct path of Buddhist faith and practice.

The joy of encountering a rare person of great character, an individual who awakens us to what we are seeking in the depths of our beings—this is the mentor-disciple relationship. The correct teaching of Buddhism is transmitted through such human bonds.

Shijo Kingo Exerted Himself Just as the Daishonin Instructed

No matter how earnestly Nichiren prays for you, if you lack faith, it will be like trying to set fire to wet tinder. Spur yourself to muster the power of faith. (WND-1, 1000–1001)

This passage [from the letter "The Strategy of the Lotus Sutra] teaches that praying based on the oneness of mentor and disciple is the heart of faith for absolute victory. Inspired by the Daishonin's triumphant return from exile on Sado, his disciple Shijo Kingo,[10] burning with fresh determination, shared Nichiren's teachings with his feudal lord, Ema. But inevitably the "three obstacles and four devils" appeared, just as Nichiren says will happen when we exert ourselves in Buddhist practice. Shijo Kingo found himself being harassed by jealous fellow retainers and fell out of favor with Lord Ema, who had been swayed by their false, defamatory accusations.

In these circumstances, Kingo put Nichiren's advice into action and continued to serve his lord with sincerity and integrity. Gradually, he regained the trust of Lord Ema, who increased Kingo's landholdings threefold. This clearly demonstrated the principles of lessening one's karmic retribution and changing poison into medicine.

At this time, some fellow samurai, resenting the favor Ema had showed Kingo, attempted to assassinate him. This letter from which this passage comes is Nichiren's response to Shijo Kingo's report that he had been attacked but had survived. Nichiren starts the letter by reminding Shijo Kingo that he had overcome this challenge because of his Buddhist practice. In this passage, he explains on an even more profound level the importance of prayer.

Naturally, as this passage indicates, the Daishonin is praying earnestly for the safety and victory of his disciple. To have such a Buddhist mentor is indeed wonderful! At the same time, he emphasizes that, from the perspective of the oneness of mentor and disciple, the disciple needs to act with the same spirit and prayer as the mentor.

Sado Exile—Government authorities, in collusion with corrupt Buddhist priests, planned but failed to execute Nichiren in September 1271. They then exiled him to Sado Island, a fate tantamount to a death sentence. But after more than two years, after he had won many new supporters there and when his predictions of internal revolt and foreign invasion came true, the government pardoned him.

Immediately before the words "No matter how earnestly Nichiren prays for you," he writes, "It is the heart that is important" (WND-1, 1000). The "heart" he talks about here, which members around the world have engraved in their lives, is "the heart of the oneness of mentor and disciple."

"I am always praying for your victory; now it is time for you to rouse strong faith"—Nichiren is saying to his disciples. Praying earnestly and persistently based on the united spirit of mentor and disciple is the key to faith that enables us to overcome any adversity. Herein also lies the key to the "strategy of the Lotus Sutra."

In contrast, if mentor and disciple are not aligned in their prayers, they will not be able to bring forth their true strength and potential. In various writings, Nichiren warns "If teacher and disciple are of different minds, they will never accomplish anything" (WND-1, 909) and "If lay believers and their teacher pray with differing minds, their prayers will be as futile as trying to kindle a fire on water" (WND-1, 795).

Infusing Our Prayers and Our Lives With the Vow for Kosen-rufu

Let us consider more deeply what it means for mentor and disciple to act with the same spirit and prayer.

What lies at the heart of the mentor's spirit and prayer? It is the mentor's vow—the great vow for kosen-rufu Nichiren made to lead all people to enlightenment.

"If you are of the same mind as Nichiren," he writes, "you must be a Bodhisattva of the Earth" (WND-1, 385). As this says, those who stand up with the same spirit as the Daishonin, taking his vow as their own, are all Bodhisattvas of the Earth. Prayer infused with a vow creates a life infused with a vow. In modern times, Presidents Makiguchi and Toda stood up for kosen-rufu in accord with this teaching and established the Soka Gakkai.

Nichiren also states, "Were they not Bodhisattvas of the Earth, they could not chant [Nam-myoho-renge-kyo]" (WND-1, 385). All of us, as Soka Gakkai members, regardless of how long we've practiced, are equally noble Bodhisattvas of the Earth— people who have emerged to spread the teachings in this Latter Day of the Law based on our vow from the remote past.

> All of us, as Soka Gakkai members, regardless of how long we've practiced, are equally noble Bodhisattvas of the Earth.

Because we all share the mission of Bodhisattvas of the Earth, we can chant Nam-myoho-renge-kyo, the essence of the Lotus Sutra. Because we chant with our vow for kosen-rufu, we can realize happiness for both ourselves and others. Because we practice Nichiren Buddhism ourselves and teach others to do the same, we can carry out our human revolution, becoming individuals who act for the benefit of others. Our prayers, originally focused on ourselves alone, naturally evolve into prayers infused with the same vow as our mentor.

This is a dramatic transformation from disciples who depend on their mentor for support to disciples who actively strive with their mentor. This differs from a religion that teaches us to seek salvation from a transcendent absolute being. The fundamental principle of Buddhism is to become a compassionate person of action committed to helping all people become happy. The path of mentor and disciple means the disciple inheriting the mentor's spirit and carrying on the mentor's efforts to build a network of awakened individuals.

The "Ticket to a Happy, Healthy Life"

The respected American Buddhist journalist Clark Strand observed that without the oneness of mentor and disciple, "the Soka Gakkai could not have become what it is today."[11] He said: "It was . . . the explanation for how, even in the face of great hardship, they [the early members in Japan] had managed to rebuild the happiness of their families and their communities after the disappointments and deprivations of the war. The [mentor-disciple] relationship was, in their minds, quite literally their ticket to a happy, healthy life."[12] He also noted: "The relationship with a mentor in the Soka Gakkai tradition is fundamentally empowering and life enhancing for the disciple."[13] He believes that there is no limit to what the Soka Gakkai can achieve in the future as long as this relationship remained alive.

Because Nichiren Buddhism bases itself on the path of mentor and disciple, we can awaken to our profound mission from the remote past; we can impact the world around us with our positive spirit and actions; and we can call forth an endless stream of capable successors into the distant future.

The Soka Gakkai is dedicated to upholding the spirit of the oneness of mentor and disciple, the very heart of Buddhism. It has revived the original humanistic ideal of religion in this corrupt and degenerate Latter Day of the Law and revealed the true value of Nichiren's Buddhism of the people on a global scale. As a result, it has won the trust of leading thinkers around the world, who see our movement as a source of great hope for the twenty-first century.

Let's each adorn each day with wonderful triumphs in our personal human revolution. And, as we continue to expand our network of precious new Bodhisattvas of the Earth, let's press ahead together on the great path of the oneness of mentor and disciple that leads to happiness and victory, and let's proudly open a grand new and exciting stage of worldwide kosen-rufu!

TWO

A Religion for the Happiness of Oneself and Others—A Drama of Joy Through Dialogue

THE AMERICAN POET WALT WHITMAN SINGS:

> Afoot and light-hearted I take to the open
> road,
>
> . . . .
>
> I think whatever I shall meet on the road
> I shall like, and whoever beholds me
> shall like me,
> I think whoever I see must be happy.[14]

Whitman's ode to humanity brims with optimism, inspiration, and joy.

This describes us all. As we walk the "open road" of Soka, we behold the blossoming of beautiful, inspiring "human flowers" (LSOC, 142), each striving to fulfill a

17

unique mission, in accord with the principle of "cherry, plum, peach, and damson" (see OTT, 200). Though we may come from different cultures, backgrounds, and walks of life, we have cultivated wonderful friendships based on mutual respect, giving rise to countless moving human dramas.

cherry, plum, peach, and damson—A phrase from Nichiren's *Record of the Orally Translated Teachings* that extols the wonder of each person's unique attributes. Just as trees bloom in their distinct ways, we each should blossom in the most natural way for us.

Our heart-to-heart encounters with fellow members create a drama of the expansion of joy. This can be seen at our meetings and activities, where new members convey their fresh resolve on starting their Buddhist practice, where youth boldly express their determination or are showered in congratulatory applause, where elderly members beam with smiles, friends vow together to change their karma, and the lively voices of children resound.

Some new members have said that they were inspired to join the Soka Gakkai because of the sincerity and concern shown by the person who introduced them, and by how that person seriously prayed for their happiness and spoke to them patiently about the practice. When new members start to practice, everyone in their local organization celebrates their hope-filled new beginning as if it were their own. The Soka Gakkai is a compassionate network dedicated to people's happiness. This is our pride as practitioners of a truly humanistic religion.

A religion that lacks the power to alleviate people's

sufferings, no matter how long its history or traditions, cannot be called a living religion. We of the Soka Gakkai, wishing to realize genuine happiness for ourselves and others, and to foster ties of trust with those around us, go out into society and share with others our convictions and experiences in faith. Such proactive efforts surely constitute the lifeblood of a humanistic religion.

One's own happiness exclusive of others is not true happiness. We cannot be happy while others suffer. Seeking happiness for oneself and others is genuine happiness. The original purpose of Buddhism and the profound wish of the Buddha is to help the suffering and enable as many people as possible to become happy.

President Makiguchi, who spoke out for justice against Japan's militarist authorities, undeterred by persecution, said:

> While there is no dispute that someone who believes [in the Mystic Law of Nam-myoho-renge-kyo] will have their prayers answered and realize benefit, this alone does not constitute bodhisattva practice. There is no such thing as a self-centered Buddha who simply accumulates personal benefit and does not work for the well-being of others. Unless we carry out bodhisattva practice, we cannot attain Buddhahood. Working for the welfare of others with the heart of a parent is the mark of both the true believer and the true practitioner.[15]

Mr. Makiguchi spoke these words in 1942, just two years before he died in prison.

Here I would like to examine the altruistic practice that lies at the heart of Mahayana Buddhism: working for the happiness of oneself and others. First, let us look at a passage from Nichiren's *The Record of the Orally Transmitted Teachings*.[16]

Bodhisattva Never Disparaging's Practice of Showing Respect to All

[Bodhisattva Never Disparaging's] bow of obeisance [is] acknowledging the fact that "self" and "others" are in fact not two different things.

For this reason, when the bodhisattva Never Disparaging makes his bow of obeisance to the four kinds of believers, the Buddha nature inherent in the four kinds of believers of overbearing arrogance bows in obeisance to the bodhisattva Never Disparaging. It is like the situation when one faces a mirror and makes a bow of obeisance: the image in the mirror likewise makes a bow of obeisance to oneself. (OTT, 165)

The Lotus Sutra describes the story of Bodhisattva Never Disparaging, who was at the beginning stages of his practice, as a model for Buddhist practice in the Latter Day. Never Disparaging greeted each person he encountered with a bow of praise and respect, saying: "I have profound reverence for you, I would never dare treat you with disparagement or arrogance. Why? Because you will all practice the bodhisattva way and will then be able to attain Buddhahood" (LSOC, 308).

But people found this aggravating and reacted hostilely, showering him with abuse, beating him with sticks, or throwing stones and tiles at him. Still, he remained undeterred; rather, he would wisely retreat to a safe distance and shout to the effect: "Even so, I respect you. You will all become Buddhas!" (see LSOC, 309). He refused to stop his practice of showing respect to everyone.

The people who rejected Never Disparaging's greeting and angrily attacked him were the four kinds of believers—monks, nuns, laymen, and laywomen—described as "overbearingly arrogant" (LSOC, 309). They are called arrogant because at the core of the refusal to accept the truth taught by the Buddha lies arrogance arising from "fundamental ignorance."

This passage from the *Orally Transmitted Teachings* employs the metaphor of a mirror. When we bow before a mirror, the image in the mirror bows back. Likewise, the Buddha nature inherent in the arrogant four

fundamental ignorance—Also, fundamental darkness or primal ignorance. The most deeply rooted illusion inherent in life, said to give rise to all other illusions. Darkness in this sense mean the inability to see or recognize the truth, particularly the true nature of one's life.

kinds of believers bows respectfully to Never Disparaging, even if the people themselves are unaware of it. From the Buddhist perspective, this is the dynamic way human life interacts in its depths. Mr. Makiguchi underlined this passage.

As we explain Buddhism to others, those who don't understand our intentions may criticize us, but we shouldn't allow that to bother us. Our sincere prayers for their happiness and our earnest efforts at dialogue will certainly reach their hearts. In the depths of our lives and theirs, our Buddha natures are greeting and urging one another to come forth.

We Are All Supremely Worthy of Respect

Bodhisattva Never Disparaging's practice of showing respect to others is the same as our practice of introducing people to Nichiren Buddhism. My mentor, Mr. Toda, always taught us that if we had problems, we should share Buddhism with others, and that in so doing, we would be able to change our own karma.

Sharing Buddhism is not about debating or defeating others in argument. It is urging another person to awaken to the fact that we are all beings worthy of supreme respect who possess the Buddha nature. Bodhisattva Never Disparaging did precisely this. It is also a struggle to break down the icy walls of darkness or ignorance in our own lives, which take the forms of apathy, passivity, and other negative emotions.

When we talk with others about Buddhism, we are grappling with our own ignorance and earthly desires. That's why it gives us the strength to surmount our own problems, enabling us to transform our state of life and change our karma. In that sense, sharing Buddhism comes down to overcoming our own cowardice, laziness, and delusion, thus enabling us to dispel the darkness or ignorance in our own lives and in the lives of others.

Buddhist dialogue isn't something we engage in only once we've attained enlightenment. Rather, such dialogue is an integral part of our Buddhist practice, which we carry out by connecting and talking with others just as the mentor teaches.

Buddhism originated in Shakyamuni's actions to communicate the truth to which he had personally awakened. His efforts to share his enlightenment began when he went to see five old friends. He conversed with them at length, and eventually one of the friends understood his message. Thereafter, others followed, one after another.

Why do we spread the Law? Shakyamuni called on his disciples: "Wander forth . . . for the welfare of the multitude, for the happiness of the multitude."[17] Our practice doesn't end with our own enlightenment; we practice to realize happiness for both ourselves and others. This is what makes Buddhism a truly humanistic religion.

> Our practice doesn't end with our own enlightenment; we practice to realize happiness for both ourselves and others.

Introducing Others to Buddhism Is the Practice of Compassion

Another passage from the *Orally Transmitted Teachings* states that Bodhisattva Never Disparaging's practice of showing respect to everyone expresses his conviction that all people possess the Buddha nature and that this conviction arises from his compassion.

Mr. Toda also declared that introducing others to Buddhism is the practice of compassion, saying: "Compassionate action is 'the work of the Buddha.' It is also truly noble because, in the process of such efforts, we not only realize lasting happiness for ourselves but can also open that possibility for others who may be suffering from poverty and want. There is, therefore, no nobler work than this."[18] Again, it is about happiness for both ourselves and others.

Mr. Toda also observed that it can be very difficult for ordinary people to bring forth compassion. He therefore taught that we can substitute courage for compassion. It takes courage to reach out and share Buddhism with others. Courage gives rise to compassionate action. Our efforts to introduce others to Buddhism always start from a courageous first step, setting in motion waves of inner transformation.

Nichiren writes, "All the Buddhas of the three existences and the ten directions have invariably attained Buddhahood through the seeds represented by the five characters of Myoho-renge-kyo"[19] (WND-1, 1015). The Mystic Law [the Law of Nam-myoho-renge-kyo] is the original cause for the enlightenment of all Buddhas. He also writes, "The Lotus Sutra is like the seed, the Buddha like the sower, and the people like the field" (WND-1, 748). Once the seed for attaining Buddhahood is sown in the lives of living beings, they are certain to attain Buddhahood. Therefore, the most important part of Nichiren Buddhist practice is sowing the seed of Buddhahood in people's lives. That practice of sowing is nothing special. It is simply reaching out to those in our lives and speaking to them, even just a few words, about the Mystic Law. It is communicating, in our own way, how wonderful the teachings of Buddhism are. This will awaken the Buddha nature inherent in all people, allowing it to sprout and blossom.

Next, I would like to discuss the significance of sowing the seed of enlightenment, based on a passage from Nichiren's work "How Those Initially Aspiring to the Way Can Attain Buddhahood through the Lotus Sutra."

Using Our Voice

Because one has heard the Lotus Sutra, which leads to Buddhahood, with this as the seed, one will invariably become a Buddha.

Thus, T'ien-t'ai[20] and Miao-lo,[21] following this principle, state in their commentaries that one should persist in preaching the Lotus Sutra. . . .

> One should by all means persist in preaching the
> Lotus Sutra and causing them to hear it. Those who
> put their faith in it will surely attain Buddhahood,
> while those who slander it will establish a "poison-
> drum relationship" with it and will likewise attain
> Buddhahood.
>
> In any event, the seeds of Buddhahood exist nowhere
> apart from the Lotus Sutra. (WND-1, 882)

The Lotus Sutra—in other words, the five characters of
Myoho-renge-kyo—is the seed of enlightenment for all
Buddhas. Consequently, this passage asserts, even a person
in the defiled age of the Latter Day who has only just aroused
faith in Buddhism will invariably attain Buddhahood upon
hearing the Lotus Sutra.

The Daishonin singles out the faculty of hearing among
the five senses because our world is a place where "one
gains the way through the faculty of hearing," he says. Just
hearing about the Lotus Sutra, the other person's voice,
is an external cause that plants the seed for attaining
Buddhahood in one's life, guaranteeing that one will attain
enlightenment and realize absolute happiness. Even if one
doesn't listen to what is being said about the Lotus Sutra,
or even if one is unable to physically hear, the "Buddha's
voice" penetrates the depths of one's being.

Talking about Nichiren Buddhism, the heart of the
Lotus Sutra, sharing the joy and conviction we've experienced through our practice, and enabling others to hear the

sound of Nam-myoho-renge-kyo being chanted—all of these actions sow the seed of enlightenment, of Buddhahood, in their lives.

People differ in their personalities and circumstances, and they all have different challenges and problems. But seen with the eyes of the Buddha, they are struggling valiantly amid the sea of the sufferings of birth, aging, sickness, and death. Wishing to share the Mystic Law—the "highly effective medicine" for all humankind (LSOC, 269)—we strive patiently to connect with each person's life.

Nichiren uses the word *persist*. This does not imply forcing the teaching upon others. Rather, it implies daring to act, seeking to create positive bonds with people. Without worrying about whether those we are talking to have the capacity to understand, and without being swayed by their reaction, we dare to reach out and talk to them about our practice and the true purpose of our movement. This is what it means to share Buddhism, the essence of which is the practice of sowing the seed of Buddhahood in people's lives.

All people have the Buddha nature, but we can't see it. We can't even see our own Buddha nature. This is a fact of being human. But we can believe the assertion that "the Buddha dwells within our hearts," just like "flint has the potential to produce fire" (WND-1, 1137). That is, we can believe that the Mystic Law is the teaching that enables all people to attain Buddhahood. It is with these eyes of faith that we need to look at people. Whether or not they heed what we say, we should persist in our sincere efforts to teach them about Buddhism.

In a letter to one of his lay followers, the Daishonin writes: "I entrust you with the propagation of Buddhism in your province. It is stated that 'the seeds of Buddhahood sprout as a result of conditions'" (WND-1, 1117). Here he stresses the importance of helping others form a connection with Buddhism so they can summon forth their Buddha nature.

The only way to awaken people's inherent Buddha nature is to sow the seed for attaining Buddhahood in their lives. This is because the Buddha nature is activated when it connects with the Mystic Law. This is why we engage in Buddhist dialogue—because it creates the best possible conditions for bringing forth the Buddha nature in people's lives. And Nichiren tells us that once sown, the seed for attaining Buddhahood will never disappear: "If one can establish a relationship with even just one phrase of the Wonderful Law [Nam-myoho-renge-kyo], that relationship will continue unbroken over a million kalpas" (OTT, 219).

Sharing Buddhism Creates Trust

Since I started practicing at age nineteen, I have shared Nichiren Buddhism with many people in my life, from family members and friends to neighbors and acquaintances. Some were responsive and some were not. One person actually returned all the letters I had written to him about Buddhism. There were times when I wondered why so few people sought Nichiren Daishonin's teachings.

But no one can avoid the sufferings of birth, aging, sickness, and death. Deep down, everyone longs for the Mystic Law, the key to overcoming these ups and downs of life. I prayed earnestly and spoke to as many people as possible, wishing to enable them to forge even a small connection with Buddhism and wishing they would become happy. Nothing brought me greater joy than when my sincere and steady efforts at dialogue resulted in someone deciding to practice Nichiren Buddhism.

But no one can avoid the sufferings of birth, aging, sickness, and death. Deep down, everyone longs for the Mystic Law, the key to overcoming these ups and downs of life.

Mr. Toda once joined me when I shared Buddhism with someone. I was deeply grateful to have a wonderful mentor who would support me in this way, inexperienced youth that I was.

"We create trust when we share Nichiren Buddhism," Mr. Toda used to say. We pray for the other person's happiness and speak with them seriously. Whether they decide to start practicing, our sincerity is sure to reach them.

I have stayed in touch with those friends I shared Nichiren Buddhism with in my youth but who didn't embrace faith. Back then, I wrote in a poem, "May you find happiness, my friend!"[22] This wish for each of them remains unchanged, even though we took different paths. All of my efforts to share Buddhism are golden treasures of my life. And those challenging experiences contributed positively to my later dialogues with world leaders and thinkers.

In the passage we are studying, Nichiren mentions a "poison-drum relationship," the idea that even those who slander or oppose the Lotus Sutra when they hear it nevertheless form a relationship with it, which ensures they will eventually attain Buddhahood. The task of spreading the Lotus Sutra—of sowing the seed for attaining Buddhahood—is to use our voices to help those around us, based on the Buddha's compassion and vow to enable all people to become happy.

In a letter to Shijo Kingo, Nichiren writes:

> The Lotus Sutra states: "If one of these good men or good women in the time after I have passed into extinction is able to secretly expound the Lotus Sutra to one person, even one phrase of it, then you should know that he or she is the envoy of the Thus Come One. He has been dispatched by the Thus Come One and carries out the Thus Come One's work." (WND-1, 331)

This passage praises those who share even a single phrase of the Lotus Sutra with another person, saying they are envoys of the Thus Come One, of the Buddha.

Wishing for the Happiness of All People

Mr. Toda wrote an editorial titled "The Benefit of Sharing Buddhism With Others" that appeared in the first issue of our organization's journal *Kachi Sozo* (Value creation) when it resumed publication after World War II (in June 1946). In its conclusion, he urged, "Whether they seem interested or not, let us do our best to help people embrace the Mystic Law and savor boundless happiness in their lives."[23]

As Japan was suffering in the aftermath of World War II, Mr. Toda, standing up alone with a great vow for kosen-rufu, was already looking far beyond the confines of his own small country and aspiring to bring happiness to people throughout the world. Now, more than seventy years later, the banner of Buddhist dialogue is flying all around the globe, in perfect accord with the image of Bodhisattvas of the Earth emerging in ever-growing numbers.

Nichiren encourages us to "teach others to the best of your ability, even if it is only a single sentence or phrase" (WND-1, 386). Without a doubt, all our efforts to fulfill the great vow for worldwide kosen-rufu and carry out our noble mission will shine as "the only memory of [our] present life in this human world" (WND-1, 64), and the development of our Soka movement will open a great road of hope that will light the way for humanity into the future.

Whatever our challenges, let us continue to sow the seeds of the Mystic Law—seeds of hope, happiness, and peace—with boundless confidence and courage!

THREE

A Teaching That Enlightens and Empowers—Faith of the Courageous Standing Alone

THE AMERICAN FUTURIST HAZEL HENDERSON once asked me why the Soka Gakkai movement had spread on such a global scale. I told her it was because we have always treasured and respected each individual.[24]

Ms. Henderson, who started out tackling various environmental problems and went on to lead numerous grassroots efforts, nodded in understanding. She has stayed true to her conviction that a genuinely popular movement must awaken each person's spirituality.[25]

Our Soka network, with members in 192 countries and territories around the world, is the fruition of our sustained efforts to meet and talk with others and help them elevate their consciousness and cultivate wisdom. Through our steadfast efforts to carry out one-to-one dialogue and encourage others, we have enabled one person after another to change themselves from within. That is why we have grown into such a vibrant socially engaged grassroots movement. This is the underlying strength of the Soka Gakkai, which has attracted the attention of people around the globe as an organization dedicated to world peace.

As the devoted disciple of my mentor, Josei Toda, I took my first step toward worldwide kosen-rufu, the cherished wish of Nichiren Daishonin, on October 2, 1960. The Cold War was intensifying, the threat of nuclear weapons was growing, and armed conflicts and civil strife were occurring around the globe. My mentor, grieved by the misery of people everywhere, entrusted us, his disciples, with the mission of illuminating the world with the light of Nichiren's Buddhism of the Sun and creating the happiness and peace humanity longed for.

Everything that happens in society is the work of human beings. For that reason, though it may seem like a roundabout route, any effort to build a brighter future must begin with a change in human beings themselves. All things, including attaining world peace and the happiness of humankind, start and end with people.

The fundamental purpose of religion is to revitalize people and enable them to lead lives of joy. What is truly needed, therefore, is a religion that teaches the worth and dignity of life and enlightens and empowers each individual. This is the essence of a religion that exists for the sake of the people rather than religion that exists solely for religion's sake.

Here I would like to focus on the principles of Nichiren Buddhism that enable us to transform our lives.

You Are Supremely Worthy!

In the Latter Day of the Law, no treasure tower exists other than the figures of the men and women who embrace the Lotus Sutra. It follows, therefore, that whether eminent or humble, high or low, those who chant Nam-myoho-renge-kyo are themselves the treasure tower, and, likewise, are themselves the Thus Come One Many Treasures. No treasure tower exists other than Myoho-renge-kyo. The daimoku of the Lotus Sutra is the treasure tower, and the treasure tower is Nam-myoho-renge-kyo. . . .

Abutsu-bo is therefore the treasure tower itself, and the treasure tower is Abutsu-bo himself. No other knowledge is purposeful. (WND-1, 299)

The Daishonin powerfully declares: You are the treasure tower! You are supremely worthy! That is the message of this passage. President Makiguchi studied this writing deeply and underlined many of its passages. It elucidates the fundamental teaching of humanism in Nichiren Buddhism, which places the highest value on the individual.

In this letter, the Daishonin extols the dignity and limitless potential of all people and clarifies the means for making the infinitely noble Buddha nature inherent in their lives shine its brightest.

In "Emergence of the Treasure Tower," the Lotus Sutra's eleventh chapter, a giant tower suddenly appears before the assembly. Mr. Toda described this ceremony as follows:

> The great and mystic life state of Buddhahood is latent within our own lives. The power and condition of this life state is beyond imagination, defying all description. Nevertheless, we can actualize it in our own lives. This ceremony of the "Treasure Tower" chapter explains that we can, in fact, bring forth the latent state of Buddhahood from within our very own lives.[26]

The Daishonin tells us that in the Latter Day of the Law, those who uphold the Mystic Law and strive earnestly in their Buddhist practice are themselves great and magnificent treasure towers. He stresses this point by saying, "No treasure tower exists other than the figures of the men and women who embrace the Lotus Sutra."

treasure tower—A tower adorned with jewels and treasures, the most famous of which appears in the Lotus Sutra. It is described as massive, thousands of miles high. Nichiren viewed the tower as an allegory for human life in its enlightened state achieved through chanting Nam-myoho-renge-kyo.

His message is that though we are all different in our appearance and physical form and in our individual circumstances, each of us who embraces the Gohonzon, chants Nam-myoho-renge-kyo, and works for kosen-rufu can—just as we are, in our present form—cause the treasure tower of life adorned with the seven kinds of treasures to shine brilliantly. This is what makes Nichiren Buddhism a universal teaching transcending all differences of nationality, ethnicity, and gender.

And not only that, the Daishonin teaches that we are all, just as we are, Many Treasures Buddha. Our efforts and behavior as we embrace the Mystic Law and engage in our Buddhist practice accord with those of Many Treasures Buddha. There are no requirements other than to "embrace the Lotus Sutra" (WND-1, 299). We don't have to do anything special.

That's why there is no need to try to be anyone other than who we are, to put on airs, or to envy others. If we have problems, all we need to do is continue striving in our faith. A way of life in which we persevere in faith, no matter what happens, and never give in to defeat itself proves our victory and testifies to the power of the Lotus Sutra.

A Clear Mirror to See the Treasure Tower Within Us

The Daishonin tells Abutsu-bo [one of his disciples on Sado Island]: "Abutsu-bo is therefore the treasure tower itself, and the treasure tower is Abutsu-bo himself. No other knowledge is purposeful." The important thing is that we strive to manifest our inner life state of Buddhahood as treasure towers of the Mystic Law.

Elsewhere, the Daishonin writes, "Since [we] believe solely in the Lotus Sutra . . . [we] can enter the treasure tower of the Gohonzon" (WND-1, 832). He inscribed the Gohonzon as a clear mirror to enable us to see our inner treasure tower.

Mr. Toda taught us: "Firmly decide that you yourself are Nam-myoho-renge-kyo." The aim of our Buddhist practice is to establish the treasure tower of Nam-myoho-renge-kyo in the depths of our lives.

The treasure tower is the life state of Buddhahood, which is revealed by vanquishing fundamental ignorance through strong prayer. It is the elemental force within life that enables us to rise up from all suffering and despair and win.

We who embrace the Gohonzon can actualize this treasure tower within our lives anytime and anywhere and transform our environment into the Land of Eternally Tranquil Light. And not only do we try to bring forth the treasure tower in our own lives, but we also help others do the same. That is the purpose of the Gohonzon and faith in Nichiren Buddhism. The keys to achieving this are the Soka path of mentor and disciple, the unity of many in body, one in mind, and the organization dedicated to realizing kosen-rufu.

Land of Eternally Tranquil Light—The Buddha land, free from impermanence and impurity. In many sutras, the world we live in is described as impure, filled with delusion and suffering, with the Buddha land being somewhere else far away. The Lotus Sutra reveals that these two lands are one and the same, determined by the purity or impurity of our minds.

The surest and most fundamental way to achieve peace is to help more and more people around the world reveal the treasure tower—their inherent dignity—in their lives.

The Commitment to Leave No One Behind

The monolithic, complex structures of contemporary society can be said to weaken the power of the individual. This can instill in people a feeling of impotence and destroy their self-esteem and self-belief, causing them to feel unworthy and lose their sense of meaning.

By becoming aware of our dignity and finding a sense of purpose and pride, we can summon invincible courage to face any challenge, no matter our circumstances. A tenacity to overcome all hardships is born within us. We can develop inner strength and fortitude. We can rise up and take on any obstacle, becoming "a person who falls to the ground, but who then pushes himself up from the ground and rises to his feet again" (WND-1, 1108).

The way we perceive our own lives is also the way we perceive the lives of others. When we have a sense of our own dignity, we recognize the dignity of others and value their lives too.

"To leave no one behind" is a core principle guiding the efforts of the global community to attain the U.N. Sustainable Development Goals.[27] This deeply resonates with the Soka Gakkai's aim to make the dignity of every individual, without exception, shine its very brightest and to bring forth the treasure tower in the lives of ourselves and others.

It is no exaggeration to say that the world today eagerly seeks a movement like ours that is based on altruistic bodhisattva practice, where individuals awakened to their own dignity strive to help others reveal the treasure tower in the depths of their lives.

"Pure Benefit Will Pour Forth"

There is nothing to lament when we consider that we will surely become Buddhas. Even if one were to become an emperor's consort, of what use would it be? Even if one were to be reborn in heaven, what end would it serve? Instead, you will follow the way of the dragon king's daughter and rank with the nun Mahaprajapati. How wonderful! How wonderful! Please chant Nam-myoho-renge-kyo, Nam-myoho-renge-kyo. (WND-1, 657)

Mr. Toda often used to say to new members:

We all have negative karma that has accumulated over countless eons from the infinite past. Our life is therefore like a garden hose clogged with debris. In the beginning, even if we bring the pure water of the world of Buddhahood to flow in our life by means of faith, it is the dirt in our life that will initially be forced out. This is why we have to struggle with our karma.

But if we continue with our Buddhist practice, then eventually pure benefit will pour forth without fail. We will definitely be able to transform our karma, or destiny, in this life—that is, we will actualize the principle of attaining Buddhahood in this lifetime. The Gohonzon is the great beneficial medicine with the tremendous power that enables us to do this. It is a supremely noble device for producing happiness.

Faith in Nichiren Buddhism enables us to become happy without fail. Encountering difficulties in the course of our Buddhist practice proves that we are progressing in changing our karma and attaining Buddhahood in this lifetime. This is absolutely assured.

In the passage we are studying from "The Bow and Arrow," a letter addressed to the lay nun Toki, the Daishonin asks rhetorically what the use is of becoming an emperor's consort, free from all wants, or of being reborn in the world of heaven. The rapturous joy of the life state of heaven—one of the Ten Worlds—is fleeting and impermanent.

Nichiren Buddhism is not a religion that seeks happiness some other place. It is a teaching that enables us to bring forth a pure, unsullied state of life amid the harsh challenges of society, a state of life that can withstand any hardship. It enables us to build enduring, indestructible happiness, just as beautiful lotus blossoms grow in muddy water.

The Daishonin encourages Toki, assuring her with absolute conviction that as one

dragon king's daughter—
When the dragon king's daughter appears in the Lotus Sutra, she is said to have already attained enlightenment. This has important implications: (1) it refutes the early Buddhist idea that women can never attain enlightenment, and (2) it reveals that all people can attain enlightenment now, in their present forms.

who upholds faith in the Mystic Law, she will follow in the footsteps of the dragon king's daughter, who opened the way to the enlightenment of all women, and attain Buddhahood without fail. He also tells her that when she attains Buddhahood in the future, she will be on a par with Mahaprajapati, Shakyamuni's stepmother and first female disciple, who the Lotus Sutra predicts will become a widely admired Buddha named Gladly Seen by All Living Beings. In addition, the Daishonin explains to Toki, who herself had long been struggling with poor health, the significance of encountering hardships and dealing with illness.

Buddhism clearly sets forth teachings that inspire hope, revealing the quintessential power for overcoming adversity. These include such principles as lessening one's karmic retribution, changing poison into medicine, and voluntarily assuming the appropriate karma. When facing difficulties, we tend to ask ourselves why this is happening to us and become caught up in our immediate suffering.

That is why in this letter the Daishonin attempts to lift up Toki's state of life.

If we view our problems or suffering simply as the result of karma from the past, then we are taking a backward approach. Instead, we need to revise our outlook and see suffering as something we have voluntarily taken on to fulfill our mission—something we have vowed to overcome through faith to demonstrate the Mystic Law's tremendous power and thereby help others achieve happiness. Faith in Nichiren Buddhism enables us to bring forth such dynamic life force. This is living with the spirit of changing karma into mission.

When awakened to our mission, we become infinitely strong. Not only can we surmount our own problems, but the story of our victory paves the way for helping many others attain Buddhahood as well. When we adopt this way of thinking, our hearts once shrouded in the darkness of suffering become filled with the light of courage and hope. Our life state expands tremendously and we become less focused on achieving our own victory alone and more focused on enabling others also to win in their lives. As a result, our lives take on a rich new meaning.

Mr. Toda used to say: "Becoming happy yourself is no great challenge; it's quite easy. But the essence of Nichiren Buddhism lies in helping others become happy too."[28] Being committed to others' well-being enables us to transform our state of life, and making efforts to encourage others is the driving force that propels our own human revolution and inspires others to do theirs.

Tapping Powerful Life Force

Nichiren Buddhism does not teach passive belief in something outside ourselves. Prayer in Nichiren Buddhism is drawing forth hope based on resolute faith. The practice of chanting Nam-myoho-renge-kyo is the source of the wisdom and power of Buddhahood. Our ability to tap great life force comes down to the strength of our faith.

> The practice of chanting Nam-myoho-renge-kyo is the source of the wisdom and power of Buddhahood.

When you're suffering, when you're sad, when you're hurting, just chant Nam-myoho-renge-kyo with an open heart. Keep chanting just as you are, as if sharing your feelings with a caring parent. In this way, you transform your problems into prayers.

Most important, as you chant, you will experience courage surging up from within, filling you with the conviction that you can triumph over what's troubling you. Even if the problem isn't resolved immediately, the time will come when "the sufferings of hell will vanish instantly" (WND-1, 199). When you look back, you'll find that the difficulty that was causing you so much heartache became an opportunity for you to make great strides in expanding your state of life. Your prayers to the Gohonzon will cause the joyous sun of your mission to rise in your heart and enable you to make your life in this existence shine with supreme brilliance.

Nothing and no one can ever rob us of the inner strength that is the life state of Buddhahood. It is invincible. That's why, while dedicating ourselves earnestly to our Buddhist practice, we should "regard both suffering and joy as facts of life" (WND-1, 681) and continue chanting Nam-myoho-renge-kyo to the Gohonzon. We need to chant tenaciously, refusing to be defeated. That spirit itself constitutes the life state of Buddhahood, and it will unmistakably be manifested as victory in the real world.

Prayers filled with conviction that powerfully activate the protective forces of the universe enable us to freely draw forth that life state from within. Those who stand up with such inner strength are true champions. Because the lives of such individuals are so dynamic and vibrant, they can impart courage and hope to everyone they encounter.

The True Strength of a Bodhisattva of the Earth

Those who have suffered the most deserve the greatest happiness. Those experiencing the harshest karma can embrace the noblest mission and fulfill it. The ancient Roman emperor Marcus Aurelius stated that the ability to lead a good life comes from within.[29] He also wrote: "Dig within. There lies the well-spring of good: ever dig, and it will ever flow."[30]

We uphold the great Buddhism of human revolution. We possess within us a reservoir of powerful, limitless resolve and tenacity to realize our goals, no matter what obstacles arise.

When Mr. Toda's businesses were in crisis,[31] I took full responsibility to support and assist him through everything. During that time, as he faced those challenges, I witnessed in his solemn and dignified demeanor the true strength of a Bodhisattva of the Earth and the real depth of humanity. Mr. Toda said, "As far as faith is concerned, I am patient to the point of obstinacy."

> People who discover a mission to which they can devote their lives without regret are free of all fear and anxiety.

People who discover a mission to which they can devote their lives without regret are free of all fear and anxiety. Being Mr. Toda's disciple has been my life's mission. Nothing can destroy the bonds of mentor and disciple dedicated to the vow of kosen-rufu. Our lives, united as one, are eternally indestructible.

To stand alone is to have absolute conviction in the nobility of your own life. It is having the inner strength to believe in your potential and live true to yourself. The Daishonin declares, "This is my vow, and I will never forsake it!" (WND-1, 281). The commitment to fulfill your vow opens the way to unlimited victories in your own life and the lives of others.

We have entered an age when our movement for worldwide kosen-rufu is advancing dynamically, when the "human flowers" of the Bodhisattvas of the Earth blossom fragrantly everywhere around the globe.

Cherishing the great vow of mentor and disciple in our hearts, as self-reliant individuals who can stand alone, let us further expand our network of champions of human revolution!

FOUR

A Religion That Connects the World—A Solidarity of "Good Friends"

THE CURRENT OF WORLDWIDE KOSEN-RUFU cannot be stopped. In 2013, the Hall of the Great Vow for Kosen-rufu was completed, and the new era of worldwide kosen-rufu began in earnest. Since then, all around the globe, courageous Bodhisattvas of the Earth, fulfilling their vow to spread the Mystic Law, have made great strides in developing our kosen-rufu movement with youth in the lead. They have made the foundation for future generations ever more solid.

The Hall of the Great Vow for Kosen-rufu

In accord with the Daishonin's words "the time makes it so" (WND-1, 736), the time has come for us to further advance our movement for worldwide kosen-rufu, which continues to flow powerfully like a mighty river.

The Soka Gakkai is the organization advancing kosen-rufu based on the life-affirming principles of Nichiren Buddhism. The aim of kosen-rufu is to bring forth the positive potential inherent in people, elevate their life state, and build a solidarity of peace and happiness.

The Soka Gakkai was founded in 1930, in the interval between two world wars, with the lofty mission of realizing lasting peace and enabling people everywhere to attain enlightenment. And the Soka Gakkai International was established in 1975, in the midst of the Cold War, when the threat of nuclear war loomed.

The eminent British historian Arnold J. Toynbee (1889–1975) wrote a foreword to an English edition of my novel *The Human Revolution*, published in 1972. In it, he states: "Already Soka Gakkai is a world affair. . . . [Nichiren's] horizon and his concern were not bounded by Japan's coasts. Nichiren held that Buddhism, as he conceived it, was a means of salvation for his fellow human beings everywhere. In working for the human revolution, Soka Gakkai is carrying out Nichiren's mandate."[32]

We have indeed entered an age when people take note of and hold high hopes for our movement of human revolution, which is now spreading throughout the world. Let us seize this opportunity and continue to engage energetically in dialogue with one person after another, moving step by step toward realizing world peace and changing the destiny of all people as we each forge happy lives.

"The Soka Gakkai Will Transform This Troubled World"

My mentor, Josei Toda, declared: "The Soka Gakkai will transform this troubled world we live in. Let's rouse our courage, unite, and forge ahead on the great path of kosen-rufu!"

Obstacles are bound to arise whenever one attempts to achieve something unprecedented. That's why we, as members of the Soka Gakkai, a noble gathering of Buddhas, need to firmly unite based on faith. Our duty is to build a citadel of kosen-rufu, of the people, and of peace that can withstand the fiercest onslaughts of the three obstacles and four devils and the three powerful enemies.

A gathering of people who correctly practice the Buddha way and spread the Buddha's teachings is called a sangha, or a harmonious community of practitioners joined together in an open and egalitarian spirit. It plays an invaluable role in helping people carry out their Buddhist practice. Today, it takes the form of an organization. An organization is indispensable for our Buddhist practice, for our efforts to attain Buddhahood in this lifetime, and to realize the goal of

three powerful enemies— Three types of arrogant people who persecute those who propagate the Lotus Sutra in the evil age after Shakyamuni's death: arrogant lay people, arrogant priests, and arrogant false sages.

kosen-rufu. The Soka Gakkai today is a sangha in the truest sense.

Here I would like to confirm the importance of our organization by referring to key passages from Nichiren Daishonin's writings.

A Dialogue Between Shakyamuni and Ananda

When a tree has been transplanted, though fierce winds may blow, it will not topple if it has a firm stake to hold it up. But even a tree that has grown up in place may fall over if its roots are weak. Even a feeble person will not stumble if those supporting him are strong, but a person of considerable strength, when alone, may fall down on an uneven path. . . .

Therefore, the best way to attain Buddhahood is to encounter a good friend. How far can our own wisdom take us? If we have even enough wisdom to distinguish hot from cold, we should seek out a good friend. (WND-1, 598)

This passage from "Three Tripitaka Masters Pray for Rain" teaches that we can overcome all difficulties and hardships with the support of "good friends."

A Buddhist scripture records an exchange between Shakyamuni and his disciple Ananda.[33] One day, Ananda asks Shakyamuni: "It seems to me that by having good friends and advancing together with them, one has already halfway attained the Buddha way. Is this way of thinking correct?" Shakyamuni responds unequivocally: "Ananda, this way of thinking is not correct. Having good friends and advancing together with them is not half the Buddha way but all the Buddha way."[34]

This describes the essence of Buddhist practice. We need to have good friends who help and support us if we are to stay on the correct path of faith and lead a life of genuine victory.

Good friends, or positive influences, are people who guide us to the correct teaching of Buddhism. They include a good teacher and good fellow practitioners. "How far can our own wisdom take us?" asks the Daishonin, stressing how important it is for us to seek out good friends in faith. The path to attaining Buddhahood is the only way to resolve the fundamental human sufferings of life and death. Only with good friends who support and encourage us can we strengthen our faith, bring forth the wisdom to become happy, and attain the ultimate life state of Buddhahood.

It is difficult to encounter good friends, who, as Nichiren notes, are "fewer than the specks of dirt one can pile on a fingernail" (WND-1, 598). At the same time, there are also "evil friends"—negative influences—who obstruct people's Buddhist practice. Elsewhere, Nichiren warns against such harmful companions, stating, "Evil friends will employ enticing words, deception and flattery and speak in a clever manner, thereby gaining control over the minds of ignorant and uninformed people and destroying the good minds that are in them" (WND-2, 221).

President Makiguchi underlined this passage in his personal copy of Nichiren's writings and urged his disciples to beware of such people.

Evil friends try to sow doubt and destroy people's faith by various subtle and devious means. And in the corrupt Latter Day of the Law, positive influences are rare while negative influences are everywhere. That's why it is great good fortune to encounter good friends and form a connection with them.

> It is great good fortune to encounter good friends and form a connection with them.

The Soka Gakkai Is a Safe Haven for All

Nichiren cites the Lotus Sutra passage "Thrust aside evil friends and associate with good companions" (WND-1, 832). We need a solid foundation of good from which we can see through evil friends and overcome obstacles.

The Soka Gakkai is directly linked to the Daishonin, founded through the selfless struggles of Presidents Makiguchi and Toda. Brimming with Nichiren's spirit to relieve the sufferings of humanity, it is a safe haven for everyone. It is a warm and humanistic organization where good friends gather and no one is left behind.

The Soka Gakkai is a fortress of ordinary people where individuals from all walks of life—regardless of gender, age, social standing, renown, or economic status—can come together as fellow human beings, just as they are, without pretense or affectation, to encourage one another, grow together, and build happy lives.

Mr. Toda often declared that the Soka Gakkai was more precious than his own life. This was his impassioned call to treasure the Soka Gakkai, the organization whose mission it is to realize the Buddha's wish of actualizing worldwide kosen-rufu on an unprecedented scale.

Mr. Toda often said to leaders: "Take care of the members! I'm counting on you! The members are the Daishonin's precious emissaries. They are Buddhas propagating the Daishonin's teachings. Do all you can to encourage and support them."

There is one point we need to bear in mind when fostering our new, younger members, and that is to always strive alongside them. Striving together is the heart of Nichiren Buddhism. Sharing a struggle is the essence of the mentor-disciple relationship. Nichiren declares: "'Joy' means that oneself and others together experience joy. . . . Both oneself and others together will take joy in their possession of wisdom and compassion" (OTT, 146). It's not enough to experience joy ourselves. Supreme joy is found in rejoicing with others and acting with wisdom and compassion together.

Many new members are doing their best to share Nichiren Buddhism with those around them. It is particularly reassuring to see our youth working together for kosen-rufu.

Many are also standing up in earnest for the first time. Behind them are the tireless efforts of numerous other members who have given their all to encourage them, chant and study with them, and take action alongside them, based on a wish to walk the great path of kosen-rufu together. Those who support others can expand their own state of life, and in turn, the capable individuals they foster will also go on to accumulate "treasures of the heart" (WND-1, 851) by following that example themselves.

It is through such a chain reaction of hope that we overcome our own problems and together joyfully achieve our human revolution.

An Eternal Formula for Victory

If the spirit of many in body but one in mind prevails among the people, they will achieve all their goals, whereas if one in body but different in mind, they can achieve nothing remarkable. The more than three thousand volumes of Confucian and Taoist literature are filled with examples. King Chou of Yin led seven hundred thousand soldiers into battle against King Wu of Chou and his eight hundred men. Yet King Chou's army lost because of disunity while King Wu's men defeated him because of perfect unity. . . . Although Nichiren and his followers are few, because they are different in body, but united in mind, they will definitely accomplish their great mission of widely propagating the Lotus Sutra. Though evils may be numerous, they cannot prevail over a single great truth [or good]. (WND-1, 618)

Let us now explore a passage from "Many in Body, One in Mind," which discusses the unity that is crucial to the success of kosen-rufu. This letter clearly sets forth the eternal formula for victory that Nichiren's disciples should always follow.

After the Daishonin moved to Mount Minobu in May 1274, propagation activities proceeded in Suruga Province[35] under the leadership of his disciple and later successor, Nikko Shonin. As a result, numerous priests and lay people of other Buddhist schools began practicing Nichiren Buddhism.

This alarmed Gyochi, the deputy chief priest of Ryusen-ji, a temple in Atsuhara Village in Suruga. With his power and influence, he contrived a plot to harrass Nichiren's followers. In this letter, Nichiren stresses the importance of the unity of "many in body, one in mind" as the key to his disciples overcoming this collusion between government authorities and priests of established Buddhist schools.

This passage begins with Nichiren stressing the importance of faith in achieving unity: "If the spirit of many in body but one in mind prevails among the people, they will achieve all their goals, whereas if one in body but different in mind, they can achieve nothing remarkable."

"Many in body" means that we are all different in appearance, personality, abilities, and qualities, while "one in mind" means that we have a shared aspiration, spirit, and purpose. In that sense, many in body, one in mind—which can also be expressed as unity in diversity—means uniting toward a shared purpose while fully respecting each person's unique qualities and individuality. "One in body, different in mind," on the other hand, means an outward appearance of uniformity but complete disunity in heart and mind.

To illustrate this principle, the Daishonin cites the examples of two figures of ancient Chinese history, King Chou of Yin and King Wu of Chou. The Yin soldiers in reality hoped for the defeat of their leader, King Chou, so according to the *Records of the Historian*,[36] they held their weapons upside down and allowed the soldiers of King Wu to advance.

Malevolent forces may form alliances based on self-interest, but in the end such alliances break apart. Whether true unity can be achieved comes down to whether we share a wish for people's happiness. A profound sense of purpose to achieve a lofty goal creates the unshakable unity of many in body, one in mind.

An Alliance United in the Cause of Good

No persecution, no matter how powerful the forces inflicting it, can destroy the "single great truth [or good]" (WND-1, 618) represented by our movement, a great alliance united in the cause of good. As long as we remain united through strong faith, we are certain to overcome all obstacles and triumph without fail.

> As long as we remain united through strong faith, we are certain to overcome all obstacles and triumph without fail.

How can we build this unity of many in body, one in mind? Striving alongside my mentor in kosen-rufu, Mr. Toda, I always chanted and took action with the resolve to be firmly united in purpose with him. Each of us needs to stand up and take the lead for kosen-rufu without waiting for someone else to do it. We need to work together with our fellow members and encourage one another as we move forward.

The "mind" of many in body, one in mind is the spirit to realize kosen-rufu, the spirit to respect our fellow members, and the spirit to remain unafraid of any opposition or obstacles, the spirit of a lion king. Ultimately, it is the spirit of the oneness of mentor and disciple.

In "The Heritage of the Ultimate Law of Life," the Daishonin writes:

All disciples and lay supporters of Nichiren should chant Nam-myoho-renge-kyo with the spirit of many in body but one in mind, transcending all differences among themselves to become as inseparable as fish and the water in which they swim. This spiritual bond is the basis for the universal transmission of the ultimate Law of life and death. Herein lies the true goal of Nichiren's propagation. When you are so united, even the great desire for widespread propagation can be fulfilled. (WND-1, 217)

The "transmission of the ultimate Law of life and death" refers to the fundamental Law of the universe, Nam-myoho-renge-kyo, being transmitted by the Buddha to all people. By chanting Nam-myoho-renge-kyo with the unity of many in body, one in mind, the Daishonin tells us, we can attain Buddhahood in this lifetime and fulfill the great desire for widespread propagation, kosen-rufu.

This entails working to create a harmonious and inclusive environment, "transcending all differences." It means cherishing one another as treasured friends who are indispensable to one another's well-being and happiness, thus becoming "as inseparable as fish and the water in which they swim." The spirit of many in body, one in mind means chanting Nam-myoho-renge-kyo with the shared goal of kosen-rufu and encouraging and supporting one another to the end.

Unity That Enhances Each Person's Unique Qualities

Some might feel this emphasis on unity means suppressing our individuality and unique personalities, but Nichiren's teaching of many in body, one in mind is completely different. Teaching that all people possess the Buddha nature, Nichiren Buddhism asserts the potential and blossoming of each individual. This is articulated through the principle of "cherry, plum, peach, and damson" (see OTT, 200), which expounds the uniqueness and beauty of all living things. Through our continuous efforts to respect each person's individuality, foster mutual growth, and reveal our potential together, we achieve the kind of unity the Daishonin describes.

It can thus be said that an organization embodying the beautiful unity of many in body, one in mind enables our individuality and unique personalities to shine ever brighter. When we develop ourselves in faith toward a shared purpose, the value of our individuality or diversity shines with special brilliance.

The Soka Gakkai's members, awakened to their mission and empowered by the support and encouragement of their friends in faith, vibrantly express their individuality as they take active roles in every area of society. Mr. Toda often used to say: "With the unity of many in body, one in mind, there is nothing we can't achieve. But without it, we'll be defeated in any endeavor, no matter what it is."

In an interview with the Soka Gakkai newspaper *Seikyo Shimbun* this year (2018), the German theologian Michael von Brück expressed high hopes for the social role of our organization. He noted that the Soka Gakkai has done many things for young people and women by giving them a place at the center of its activities. He also observed that it encourages ordinary people to participate and become a force in society, which has led it to be criticized. But without such a force, he added, nothing will ever change.[37]

All around the globe, the Soka Gakkai demonstrates the vibrant energy of unity in diversity, its members transcending ethnic, cultural, and linguistic barriers. In discussion meetings, in particular, wonderful flowers of friendship and trust blossom as each person reveals their unique potential. Professor Brück has attended a few Soka Gakkai discussion meetings and said they resonated with him. He especially commended the active role taken by women in these gatherings.

Our philosophy of many in body, one in mind is certain to continue to create value everywhere as a guiding principle for promoting peace and harmony for humanity. Fostering global citizens who help one another grow and develop, forming a community of good friends, will lead to enduring peace and a secure future for global society.

Moving Ahead Together in the Soka Gakkai

Because we strive together in the unity of many in body, one in mind based on our vow for kosen-rufu, each of us can achieve our human revolution. By working to expand our movement dedicated to the cherished hope of lasting peace, we transform the karma or destiny of our countries and all humankind. Creating hope is the Soka Gakkai's mission.

Setting our sights on scaling anew the summit of kosen-rufu, let us move ahead together as we write a wonderful record of great triumph!

FIVE

Soka Religious Revolution—
The Brilliance of
Humanism Spreading
Around the Globe

P RESIDENT TODA DECLARED, "KOSEN-RUFU
is a religious revolution to enable people around the
world to become happy." The "revolution" he called for is
one free from the violence and bloodshed often associated
with the word. Rather, it expressed his extraordinary determination to help people achieve true happiness through
their own human revolution and contribute to making a
peaceful society. Mr. Toda stressed this point to us, his
youthful disciples, numerous times.

Religious revolution is nothing other than human
revolution. This is because it starts with the inner transformation of each person's life. Buddhism aims to enable
all people to change their karma or destiny and bring forth
power and potential that is as vast as the universe itself.
The human revolution of a single individual can change the

world. This, Mr. Toda taught me, is the essence of genuine religious revolution.

My two novels, *The Human Revolution* and *The New Human Revolution*, have as their theme this message of my mentor, which I embraced as my own: "A great human revolution in just a single individual will help achieve a change in the destiny of a nation and, further, will enable a change in the destiny of all humankind."

The Buddhism of the People—
Opening the Way for All
to Attain Buddhahood

Since its founding (in 1930), the Soka Gakkai has resolutely carried out a religious revolution. The compulsory *danka*, or temple parishioner, system[38] enforced in Japan during the Edo period (1603–1868), had caused the original spirit of Buddhism to be lost. It reduced it to an empty shell. In response, Mr. Makiguchi gave his all to reviving the heart of Nichiren Buddhism in modern times. He declared that "Religious reform is not difficult."[39]

The Soka Gakkai's religious reformation sought to revitalize the spirit of widespread propagation in Nichiren Shoshu [the school of Buddhism the Soka Gakkai was once allied with]. This was at a time when the Nichiren Shoshu priesthood had lost sight of the heart of Nichiren's teachings and the admonitions of his direct successor, Nikko Shonin.[40] The Soka Gakkai aimed to restore the pure flow of Buddhism by returning to the spirit of helping people become happy.

From its earliest days, therefore, the Soka Gakkai has been dedicated to advancing kosen-rufu based on harmonious unity and has carried out a Buddhist renaissance movement to repudiate religious authoritarianism and restore the original spirit of Nichiren Buddhism.

Looking back, we see that Buddhism originated in Shakyamuni's efforts to transform the prevailing trend in which people served the interests of religion into one in which religion served the interests of the people. As the centuries passed and Buddhism itself lost this original spirit, many Buddhist teachers returned to the question of what religion's true purpose is and sought to reform Buddhism as a religion dedicated to human happiness. This is the history of Buddhism as a humanistic teaching.

And in the Latter Day of the Law, an age when the Buddha's correct teaching had all but perished, Nichiren's Buddhism of the Sun appeared. Returning to the Lotus Sutra, the essence of Shakyamuni's teachings, it achieved an unprecedented religious revolution, establishing itself as the Buddhism of the people, opening the way for everyone to attain Buddhahood.

Enabling the Dignity of Each Individual to Shine

The Soka Renaissance we have carried out at the cusp of the twenty-first century can be seen as inevitable in light of this history of Buddhism. The Soka Gakkai struggled to break free from the fetters of authoritarianism and make the dignity of each individual shine. This enabled it to spread its wings and soar into the world as the humanistic religious movement people everywhere had been seeking.

Soka Renaissance— In a notice dated November 28, 1991, Nichiren Shoshu excommunicated the Soka Gakkai, and that date has since then been considered our Spiritual Independence Day. The day marked a fresh start in the organization's efforts for worldwide kosen-rufu.

Today, in this new era of worldwide kosen-rufu, our noble members throughout Japan and around the globe, firmly united in purpose, are achieving wonderful victories through their human revolution, thus contributing to the growth of our movement.

And now, many new Bodhisattvas of the Earth, linked by deep karmic ties, have joined our ranks with fresh resolve at this significant time as we set forth energetically toward our ninetieth anniversary in 2020.

Together with you, my friends who possess a wondrous mission, I would like to examine the true meaning of our Soka religious reformation based on passages from Nichiren's writings.

The Way of Life of a Wise Person

The heart of the Buddha's lifetime of teachings is the Lotus Sutra, and the heart of the practice of the Lotus

Sutra is found in the "Never Disparaging" chapter. What does Bodhisattva Never Disparaging's profound respect for people signify? The purpose of the appearance in this world of Shakyamuni Buddha, the lord of teachings, lies in his behavior as a human being.

Respectfully.

The wise may be called human, but the thoughtless are no more than animals. (WND-1, 851–52)

Buddhism is a humane teaching. A Buddha is nothing but a human being who embodies the Law. The Law does not exist anywhere apart from the actions of human beings. That is why Buddhism emphasizes a person's behavior and state of life.

In this passage from "The Three Kinds of Treasure," Nichiren reveals the way of life of a wise person. He tells Shijo Kingo, one of his most trusted and devoted followers, that the essence of Buddhism is found in our behavior as human beings. The foundation for any genuine religious reformation lies in each person's inner transformation, achieved through actions grounded in respect for others.

Shijo Kingo was facing his greatest hardship when Nichiren sent him this letter. His relationship with his feudal lord, Ema, had become severely strained due to malicious false accusations fellow samurai had made against him. Lord Ema pressed Shijo Kingo to write an oath renouncing his faith in Nichiren's teachings;

otherwise, he would confiscate his landholdings. These events took place several months before Shijo Kingo received this letter.[41]

But Shijo Kingo vowed to the Daishonin that he would never abandon his faith in the Lotus Sutra, no matter the consequences. His profound determination activated the protective forces of the universe, and Shijo Kingo, who was well versed in medicine, regained his lord's trust after treating his illness. The Daishonin wrote this letter in response to Shijo Kingo's joyous report on the dramatic change in his situation.

Throughout this lengthy letter, Nichiren explains how to behave as a human being and sets forth guiding principles for practitioners of his teaching. Though you may have regained your lord's trust, he tells his disciple, never boast about it. Always behave with sincerity and humility, he says. And he warns him that his jealous colleagues who seek his downfall are sure to be seething, so he must remain vigilant and act with prudence.

> True victory is winning trust and praise through one's behavior as a member of society and as a Buddhist practitioner.

The Daishonin further tells Kingo that true victory is winning trust and praise through one's behavior as a member of society and as a Buddhist practitioner. He urges him to live with the conviction that "the treasures of the heart are the most valuable of all" (WND-1, 851).

Teaching the Practice of Showing Respect to Others

At the close of this letter, the Daishonin says that the purpose of Shakyamuni's appearance was to preach the Lotus Sutra. He explains that the Lotus Sutra is "the heart of the Buddha's lifetime of teachings . . . , and the heart of the practice of the Lotus Sutra is found in the 'Never Disparaging' chapter."

"Bodhisattva Never Disparaging," the sutra's twentieth chapter, explains the practice of Never Disparaging. He firmly believed that all living beings possess the Buddha nature, and he persisted in paying reverence to them, no matter how he was persecuted. Nichiren thus concludes that Shakyamuni appeared in this world to teach this practice of showing respect for others through one's actions.

In other words, in this letter the Daishonin repeatedly stresses to Shijo Kingo the importance of behaving with sincerity and integrity at all times in order to triumph over his challenges.

Let us further explore what it means to act with respect for all people.

Why did Nichiren go so far as to declare that Shakyamuni's "behavior as a human being" was the purpose of his appearance in this world? No doubt because he himself embodied the philosophy of respect for life and all people that pulses vibrantly in the Lotus Sutra.

The Lotus Sutra teaches that all people have the Buddha nature. As such, everyone is equal and each person's life is infinitely worthy of respect. Based on this absolute conviction, despite arrogant people showering him with curses and abuse and attacking him with sticks and stones, Bodhisattva Never Disparaging continued to believe in them and show them respect. As a result, he received the benefit of the "purification of the six sense organs," transformed his karma, and attained the expansive life state of Buddhahood.

In other words, to always act respectfully toward others, no matter who they are, out of an unwavering belief in everyone's Buddha nature—that behavior is itself the fundamental cause for attaining Buddhahood.

The Daishonin sent warm and compassionate letters to his followers, including those he never met, demonstrating his sincere care and encouraging them with his whole heart.

At the same time, determined to lead all people in the Latter Day to happiness, he fought bravely against erroneous teachings and negative forces that caused people to suffer. He warmly supported each person while boldly remonstrating with the authorities. All these actions were rooted in compassion. His life was indeed the embodiment of showing respect to all people at all times. Now, the mentors and disciples of Soka carry on Nichiren's model of behavior and put it into action in their daily lives.

Praying for a Tranquil Society
and a Peaceful World

Because we believe in everyone's inherent Buddha nature and respect the dignity of their lives, we behave with sincerity and integrity. We also actively engage in society to build a peaceful age in which honest, decent people can lead happy lives. In "On Establishing the Correct Teaching for the Peace of the Land," the Daishonin writes, "If you care anything about your personal security, you should first of all pray for order and tranquillity throughout the four quarters of the land, should you not?" (WND-1, 24). In that spirit, we bravely rise to the challenge of doing our human revolution and transforming society.

We believe in the limitless potential of each individual.

We deeply treasure the person in front of us.

And we together demonstrate our immense capacities.

Our noble way of life accords with the true spirit of Nichiren Buddhism, and the genuine respect we show to others creates a ripple effect in our environment. We have clearly demonstrated to people throughout Japan and the world that, by taking personal responsibility and acting of our own free will, we can, with strength and wisdom, open the way to happiness and victory.

Let us proudly tell others of the modern religious reformation we have undertaken to break free of empty formalism and authoritarianism.

The Buddhism of the Sun Flourishes in the Latter Day

The moon appears in the west[42] and sheds its light eastward, but the sun rises in the east and casts its rays to the west. The same is true of Buddhism. It spread from west to east in the Former and Middle Days of the Law, but will travel from east to west in the Latter Day.[43] (WND-1, 401)

Soka Gakkai members ground their actions in respect for all people, which is the correct path of Buddhist practice. Committed to this, the Soka Gakkai today continues its religious reformation, spreading Nichiren Buddhism, the Buddhism of the people, around the world.

It was in his "On the Buddha's Prophecy" that the Daishonin predicts an age of the worldwide spread of Buddhism. In it, he writes that he is the only person fulfilling Shakyamuni's prediction that the Law would be spread widely in the Latter Day. He then makes his own prediction that the great teaching of Nam-myoho-renge-kyo, the essence of the Lotus Sutra, will eventually make its way around the globe. This worldwide spread of Nichiren's Buddhism of the Sun, with its teaching of respect for all people, is essentially what is meant by the statement that "[Buddhism] will travel from east to west in the Latter Day."

In the summer of 1951, the year Mr. Toda was inaugurated as second Soka Gakkai president, the Soka Gakkai's monthly study journal, the *Daibyakurenge*, published his article titled "The History and Conviction of the Soka Gakkai." In it, he referred to this passage from "On the Buddha's Prophecy" and spoke of his conviction and joy at being able to spread the Mystic Law in the Latter Day.

Affirming his unshakable belief that Nichiren Buddhism of the people would spread throughout Asia and the rest of the world, he wrote: "Having encountered this auspicious time, we of the Soka Gakkai have made a great vow of selfless devotion and stood up with the powerful conviction that we must engage in a momentous effort to spread the Mystic Law. How fortunate we are to advance on this path that leads to Buddhahood and allows us to savor the joy of living!"[44]

Mr. Toda clarified the Daishonin's prediction of the "westward transmission of Buddhism" to mean realizing kosen-rufu in Asia and the rest of the world, and he entrusted the actualization of that goal to the youth. Immediately after I, his devoted disciple, was inaugurated as third president (in 1960), I began my journey for worldwide kosen-rufu, Mr. Toda's photograph tucked into my breast pocket. I visited countries around the world, chanting Nam-myoho-renge-kyo as if to permeate the ground in every place I went to call forth Bodhisattvas of the Earth.

Today, our humanistic network of Soka has spread to 192 countries and territories. The chanting of Nam-myoho-renge-kyo resounds somewhere on this planet twenty-four hours a day, 365 days a year.

In "On Repaying Debts of Gratitude," the Daishonin writes, "In Japan, China, India, and all the other countries of Jambudvipa [the entire world], every person, regardless of whether wise

> The chanting of Nam-myoho-renge-kyo resounds somewhere on this planet twenty-four hours a day, 365 days a year.

or ignorant, will set aside other practices and join in the chanting of Nam-myoho-renge-kyo" (WND-1, 736). With these words engraved in our hearts, we of the Soka Gakkai have opened the way for the widespread propagation of the Mystic Law.

In *The Record of the Orally Transmitted Teachings*, the Daishonin says, "Sanskrit and Chinese join in a single moment to form Nam-myoho-renge-kyo"[45] (OTT, 4). The Daishonin is suggesting that the teaching of Nam-myoho-renge-kyo will spread in both East and West—represented in this passage by the languages of India and China—and reach all humankind.

Today, in every corner of the world, people revitalize their lives through their Buddhist practice and the beneficial power of chanting Nam-myoho-renge-kyo. Their humanistic behavior touches those around them, while the joy they experience through their practice spreads, inspiring others to stand up in faith as well. This exemplifies the "benefit of the fiftieth hearer" in a continuous chain reaction of joy as Buddhism spreads from one person to the next. We have been able to spread this movement of human revolution because we have carried out a modern religious reformation.

An Elevated Humanity

Shin Anzai (1923–98), the late Japanese scholar of religion and professor emeritus at Sophia University in Tokyo, said: "Among the writings of Nichiren Daishonin, there are numerous letters written to nameless ordinary women living in rural areas in which he offers highly detailed and compassionate encouragement and guidance. Instead of dogma, these letters overflow with a deep and rich humanity. I have witnessed the same elevated humanity among many Soka Gakkai members."[46] I am profoundly grateful for his deep understanding of our movement.

Dr. Anzai also observed: "In recent years, the Soka Gakkai has begun to walk a new path as a lay religious organization separate from the priesthood. I view this as an inevitable result of the fundamental difference between the open, progressive Soka Gakkai and the closed, conservative priesthood. The priesthood has become an anachronism, showing no appreciation of the value of peace, culture, and education, clinging to hidebound traditions and attempting to control lay followers through clerical authority and power. Had the Soka Gakkai not claimed its independence from the priesthood, it would have eventually been fated to become a self-righteous and closed religious organization, too, its bright future and global outlook perishing."[47]

As Dr. Anzai and many other leading thinkers have noted, our religious reformation has been a process of severing the chains of the authoritarian, dogmatic, and closed-minded Nichiren Shoshu priesthood and establishing spiritual independence, through each member standing up with lionlike strength and courage.

Since our spiritual independence, the Soka Gakkai's humanistic ideals have spread around the world. Our organizations in places such as Spain and Indonesia, where members suffered terribly during the trouble with the priesthood, have since experienced tremendous growth.

More than a quarter century since our Spiritual Independence Day, members in Spain, striving valiantly in the spirit of the oneness of mentor and disciple and many in body, one in mind, have increased their membership sixty-fold. Soka Gakkai Indonesia has grown from one to twelve headquarters organizations and forty-nine chapters. Members in both nations are building trust and friendship in their communities and society. The development of kosen-rufu in countries and territories worldwide is gaining widespread praise.

Our members around the world, through their behavior as human beings, are carrying out the great movement of religious reformation that is kosen-rufu. People everywhere long to encounter the humanistic teachings of Nichiren Buddhism.

Our Movement of Soka Humanism

We have entered an age when our humanistic behavior is contributing to the realization of peace and a more humane world. Our movement of Soka humanism shines ever more brightly upon the stage of the twenty-first century.

The victory of each one of you, my trusted friends, in achieving your own human revolution is the victory of the Soka Gakkai, which as a religion is being practiced around the world illuminating humanity. Let us continue moving forward in our shared struggle of mentor and disciple based on the unity of many in body, one in mind, and let's embrace the world with the great light of our Soka Renaissance!

—With prayers for the brilliant achievements
of my fellow members everywhere

NOTES

Chapter 1: A Teaching of Mentor and Disciple—Let's Walk the Path to Happiness Together

1. Yubari Coal Miners Union Incident: A case of blatant religious discrimination that took place in 1957, in which miners in Yubari, Hokkaido, were threatened with losing their jobs on account of their belonging to the Soka Gakkai.

2. Osaka Incident: The occasion when Daisaku Ikeda, then Soka Gakkai youth division chief of staff, was arrested and wrongfully charged with election law violations in a House of Councillors by-election in Osaka in 1957. At the end of the court case, which continued for more than four years, he was fully exonerated of all charges on January 25, 1962.

3. Daisaku Ikeda, *The Human Revolution*, Book 1 (Santa Monica, CA: World Tribune Press, 2004), viii.

4. This chapter was written in the summer of 2018, and the last installment of *The New Human Revolution* was published in Japanese in November 2018.

5. Many Treasures: A Buddha depicted in the Lotus Sutra. Many Treasures appears, seated within his treasure tower, in order to lend credence to Shakyamuni's teachings in the sutra. According to "Treasure Tower," the sutra's eleventh chapter, Many Treasures Buddha lives in the World of Treasure Purity in the east. While still engaged in bodhisattva practice, he pledges that, even after entering nirvana, he will appear with his treasure tower in order to attest to the validity of the Lotus Sutra, wherever it might be taught.

6. Sairen-bo: A former priest of the Tendai school of Buddhism who, for an unknown reason, had been exiled to Sado. There, he met Nichiren Daishonin and converted to his teachings.

7. Voice-hearer disciples—Shakyamuni Buddha's disciples who listen to his preaching and strive to attain enlightenment. The world of voice-hearers, or learning, is the seventh of the Ten Worlds.

8. Translated from Japanese. Article in the *Seikyo Shimbun*, August 18, 1993.

9. Translated from Japanese. Article in the *Seikyo Shimbun*, August 18, 1993.

10. Shijo Kingo (c. 1230–1300): One of Nichiren Daishonin's leading followers. His full name and title were Shijo Nakatsukasa Saburo Saemon-no-jo Yorimoto. As a samurai retainer, he served the Ema family, a branch of the ruling Hojo clan. Shijo Kingo was well versed in both medicine and the martial arts. He is said to have converted to the Daishonin's teachings around 1256. When the Daishonin was taken to Tatsunokuchi to be beheaded in 1271, Shijo Kingo accompanied him, resolved to die by his side.

11. Clark Strand, *Waking the Buddha: How the Most Dynamic and Empowering Buddhist Movement in History Is Changing Our Concept of Religion* (Santa Monica, CA: Middleway Press, 2014), 117.

12. Strand, *Waking the Buddha*, 129.

13. Strand, *Waking the Buddha*, 129.

Chapter 2: A Religion for the Happiness of Oneself and Others—A Drama of Joy Through Dialogue

14. Walt Whitman, "Song of the Open Road," *Leaves of Grass* (New York: J. M. Dent and Sons, 1968), 125–27.

15. Translated from Japanese. Tsunesaburo Makiguchi, *Makiguchi Tsunesaburo zenshu* (The collected writings of Tsunesaburo Makiguchi) (Tokyo: Daisanbunmei-sha, 1987), 10:151.

16. *The Record of the Orally Transmitted Teachings:* Nichiren Daishonin's oral teachings on the Lotus Sutra, recorded and compiled by his disciple and successor, Nikko Shonin.

17. Bhikkhu Bodhi, trans. *The Connected Discourses of the Buddha: A Translation of the Samyutta Nikaya* (Boston: Wisdom Publishing, 2000), 198.

18. Translated from Japanese. Josei Toda, *Toda Josei zenshu* (The collected writings of Josei Toda) (Tokyo: Seikyo Shimbunsha, 1981), 1:96.

19. Five characters of Myoho-renge-kyo: Myoho-renge-kyo is written with five Chinese characters, while Nam-myoho-renge-kyo is written with seven (*nam*, or *namu*, being comprised of two characters). The Daishonin often uses Myoho-renge-kyo synonymously with Nam-myoho-renge-kyo in his writings.

20. T'ien-t'ai (538–97): Also known as Chih-i. The founder of the T'ien-t'ai school in China. Commonly referred to as the Great Teacher T'ien-t'ai. His lectures were compiled in such works as *The Profound Meaning of the Lotus Sutra*, *The Words and Phrases of the Lotus Sutra*, and *Great Concentration and Insight*. He spread the Lotus Sutra in China and established the doctrine of three thousand realms in a single moment of life.

21. Miao-lo (711–82): A patriarch of the T'ien-t'ai school in China. He is revered as the school's restorer. His commentaries on T'ien-t'ai's three major works are titled *The Annotations on "The Profound Meaning of the Lotus Sutra," The Annotations on "The Words and Phrases of the Lotus Sutra,"* and *The Annotations on "Great Concentration and Insight."*

22. Daisaku Ikeda, "Morigasaki Beach," *Journey of Life: Selected Poems of Daisaku Ikeda* (London: I. B. Tauris, 2014), 7.

23. Toda, *Toda Josei zenshu*, 1:302.

Chapter 3: A Teaching That Enlightens and Empowers—Faith of the Courageous Standing Alone

24. See Hazel Henderson and Daisaku Ikeda, *Planetary Citizenship: Your Values, Beliefs, and Actions Can Shape a Sustainable World* (Santa Monica, CA: Middleway Press, 2004), 46–47.

25. Henderson, *Planetary Citizenship*, 173.

26. Translated from Japanese. Josei Toda, *Toda Josei zenshu* (The collected writings of Josei Toda) (Tokyo: Seikyo Shimbunsha, 1986), 6:275.

27. The Sustainable Development Goals were adopted by a United Nations summit as development goals for the world from 2016 to 2030. It consists of seventeen goals for realizing sustainable development and includes the pledge to leave no one behind. SGI supports these goals through a variety of initiatives. See sustainabledevelopment.un.org/sdgs for more information.

28. Translated from Japanese. Josei Toda, *Toda Josei zenshu* (The collected writings of Josei Toda) (Tokyo: Seikyo Shimbunsha, 1984), 4:378.

29. See Marcus Aurelius, *Meditations,* trans. by Maxwell Staniforth (London: Penguin Books, 1964), 171.

30. Aurelius, *Meditations*, 115.

31. In the early postwar years, Josei Toda was the sole financial supporter of the Soka Gakkai, using the income from his businesses: first a publishing company and then a credit union. In the difficult economy of those years, his ventures fell into a period of decline. Many employees deserted him, except for a young Daisaku Ikeda, who had begun to work for Toda in 1949. In 1951, with his business troubles behind him, Toda became the second Soka Gakkai president.

Chapter 4: A Religion That Connects the World—A Solidarity of "Good Friends"

32. Daisaku Ikeda, *The Human Revolution* (Tokyo: Weatherhill, 1972), 1:xi–xii (Foreword by Arnold Toynbee).

33. Ananda: One of Shakyamuni's ten major disciples. He was a cousin of Shakyamuni and also the younger brother of Devadatta. For many years he accompanied Shakyamuni as his personal attendant and thus heard more of his teachings than any other disciple. He was known, therefore, as the foremost in hearing the Buddha's teachings. In addition, he is said to have possessed an excellent memory, which allowed him to play a central role in compiling Shakyamuni's teachings at the First Buddhist Council after the Buddha's passing.

34. See Bhikkhu Bodhi, *The Connected Discourses of the Buddha: A Translation of the Samyutta Nikaya* (Boston: Wisdom Publishing, 2000), "Maggasamyutta" [2 (2) Half the Holy Life], 1524.

35. Suruga Province is in present-day central Shizuoka Prefecture.

36. *Records of the Historian:* Historical work by Ssu-ma Ch'ien (Sima Qian: 145–87 BCE). China's first comprehensive history, it was used as a model for later chronicles. The work describes the history from the legendary ruler Huang Ti (Yellow Emperor) through Emperor Wu of the Han dynasty (206 BCE–220 CE), when Ssu-ma Ch'ien lived.

37. Translated from Japanese. Article in the *Seikyo Shimbun,* March 24, 2018.

Chapter 5: Soka Religious Revolution—The Brilliance of Humanism Spreading Around the Globe

38. *Danka* system: Under this system, which was introduced by the Tokugawa military government in the mid-seventeenth century as part of its drive to eradicate Christianity in Japan, Buddhist temples were effectively turned into arms of the government bureaucracy and empowered with authority over *danka* or families living in the assigned district of a temple. It was compulsory for all households to register with a temple. This led to Buddhism becoming increasingly formalistic. Literally, *dan* means donation and *ka*, family. *Danka* means families that support a temple financially. *Danto* means individual members of the *danka*.

39. Translated from Japanese. Tsunesaburo Makiguchi, "Shukyo kaikaku zosa nashi" (Religious reform is not difficult), in *Makiguchi Tsunesaburo zenshu* (The collected writings of Tsunesaburo Makiguchi) (Tokyo: Daisanbunmeisha, 1987), 10:23–27.

40. Admonitions of Nikko Shonin: This refers to "The Twenty-Six Admonitions of Nikko," a document that Nikko Shonin, Nichiren Daishonin's designated successor, wrote for the sake of both priests and laity of future generations to maintain the purity of the Daishonin's teachings. It outlines the fundamental spirit of faith, practice, and study.

41. Lord Ema's threat to Shijo Kingo was triggered by incidents surrounding a debate held in Kuwagayatsu, Kamakura, in 1277, between the Daishonin's disciple Sammi-bo and a priest named Ryuzo-bo, who was under the patronage of Ryokan of Gokuraku-ji temple. Ryuzo-bo was thoroughly defeated by Sammi-bo. Shijo Kingo merely attended the debate as an observer, and did not utter a word. However, it was alleged to Lord Ema that he had burst into the debate with a number of confederates with weapons drawn and disrupted the proceedings. This led to Lord Ema's order that Shijo Kingo either write out a pledge saying that he had given up his practice of the Lotus Sutra or relinquish his landholdings.

42. "Moon appears in the west": This refers to the fact that the new moon is first seen in the west just after sunset. On successive nights, as the moon grows fuller, it appears to have moved a little farther toward the east. Of course, the direction of the moon's movement is from east to west, the same as that of the sun and stars, but because of its orbital motion, it appears each day to have moved slightly in retrograde, from west to east.

43. "Buddhism traveling from east to west": This is referred to as "the westward transmission of Buddhism."

44. Translated from Japanese. Josei Toda, *Toda Josei zenshu* (The collected writings of Josei Toda) (Tokyo: Seikyo Shimbunsha, 1983), 3:128.

45. "The *nam[u]* of Nam-myoho-renge-kyo is a Sanskrit word, while *myoho, renge,* and *kyo* are Chinese words" (OTT, 3).

46. Translated from Japanese. Article in the *Seikyo Shimbun*, July 28, 2002.

47. Article in the *Seikyo Shimbun*, July 28, 2002.

GLOSSARY

benefit of the fiftieth hearer—A phrase from "The Benefits of Responding with Joy," the Lotus Sutra's eighteenth chapter. A person hears the teaching of the Lotus Sutra, or Nam-myoho-renge-kyo, and rejoices. That person then tells another, who in turn rejoices and shares the joy with another on down to the fiftieth person. This passage affirms that even the last person in the chain will receive immense benefit.

Bodhisattvas of the Earth—An innumerable host of bodhisattvas who, in the Lotus Sutra, emerge from beneath the earth and to whom Shakyamuni Buddha entrusts the propagation of the Mystic Law, the essence of the Lotus Sutra. Nichiren identified himself with the leader of these bodhisattvas and regarded his followers who embrace and propagate Nam-myoho-renge-kyo as Bodhisattvas of the Earth.

Buddhahood—Buddhahood is a state of indestructible happiness, wherein we manifest limitless potential, boundless wisdom, and infinite compassion and create value out of any situation in life. A Buddha is not a supernatural being but rather an ordinary person enlightened to the eternal and ultimate truth that is the reality of all things, and who leads others to attain the same enlightenment. The Lotus Sutra reveals that all living beings have the potential for Buddhahood.

changing poison into medicine—The principle that a life dominated by the three paths of earthly desires, karma, and suffering can be transformed into a life replete with the three virtues of the Dharma body, wisdom, and emancipation by virtue of the power of the Mystic Law. In other words, any adverse situation can be changed into a positive one through the power of Buddhist practice. This phrase is found in a passage from Nagarjuna's *Treatise on the Great Perfection of Wisdom*, which mentions "a great physician who can change poison into medicine."

cherry, plum, peach, and damson—A phrase from Nichiren's *Record of the Orally Translated Teachings* that extols the wonder of each person's unique attributes. Just as trees bloom in their distinct ways, we each should blossom in the most natural way for us.

daimoku—Literally, "title," it refers to the chanting of Nam-myoho-renge-kyo. Myoho-renge-kyo is the title of the Lotus Sutra in Japanese.

dragon king's daughter—When the dragon king's daughter appears in the Lotus Sutra, she is said to have already attained enlightenment. This has important implications: (1) it refutes the early Buddhist idea that women can never attain enlightenment, and (2) it reveals that all people can attain enlightenment now, in their present forms.

four virtues—Four noble qualities of a Buddha's life: eternity, happiness, true self, and purity. These describe the true nature of a Buddha's life, which is pure and eternal and which manifests the true self and enjoys absolute happiness.

fundamental ignorance—Also, fundamental darkness or primal ignorance. The most deeply rooted illusion inherent in life, said to give rise to all other illusions. Darkness in this sense mean the inability to see or recognize the truth, particularly the true nature of one's life.

human revolution—Josei Toda, the Soka Gakkai's second president, used the term *human revolution* to describe the process of attaining Buddhahood, a self-transformation achieved through Nichiren Buddhist practice within the SGI. This transformation involves breaking the shackles of our ego-centered "lesser selves" and revealing our "great selves," wherein we experience deep compassion and joyfully take action for the sake of others, and ultimately, all humanity.

kalpa—In ancient Indian cosmology, an extremely long period of time. There are various definitions, including the time it would take to wear away a rock 450 meters on each side by brushing it with a piece of cloth once every hundred years. Another description says a kalpa is about sixteen million years.

kosen-rufu—A term from the Lotus Sutra that literally means to declare and spread widely. It refers to the process of securing lasting peace and happiness for all humankind by establishing the humanistic ideals of Nichiren Buddhism in society.

Latter Day of the Law—The last of three periods—Former Day of the Law, Middle Day of the Law, and Latter Day of the Law—following Shakyamuni's death, when his teachings are said to fall into confusion and lose the power to lead people to enlightenment. In an earlier sutra, Shakyamuni says that in this age his teachings will "be lost and obscured" and erroneous views will prevail. In the Lotus Sutra, Shakyamuni explains that the Latter Day will be the time when the Lotus Sutra will be propagated widely.

Land of Eternally Tranquil Light—The Buddha land, free from impermanence and impurity. In many sutras, the world we live in is described as impure, filled with delusion and suffering, with the Buddha land being somewhere else far away. The Lotus Sutra reveals that these two lands are one and the same, determined by the purity or impurity of our minds.

lessening one's karmic retribution—This term, which literally means "transforming the heavy and receiving it lightly," appears in the Nirvana Sutra. As a benefit of protecting the correct teaching of Buddhism, we can experience relatively light karmic retribution in this lifetime, thereby expiating heavy karma that ordinarily would adversely affect us not only in this lifetime but over many lifetimes to come.

Nichiren Shoshu—One of the Nichiren sects in Japan, with whom the Soka Gakkai was allied from 1930 to 1991. After World War II, the Soka Gakkai grew into a substantial worldwide movement with a membership of several million. The priesthood of Nichiren Shoshu found itself ill prepared to deal with an active and socially engaged membership body of this scale. Its sixty-seventh chief priest, Nikken, sought to disband the Soka Gakkai and bring its membership under his direct control. The Soka Gakkai resisted this plan, as well as the priesthood's claim that the chief priest had special powers, and was excommunicated in 1991. The Soka Gakkai has continued to grow and flourish and now has members in 192 countries and territories.

poison-drum relationship—Poison-drum relationship: A reverse relationship, or a relationship formed through rejection. A bond formed with the Lotus Sutra by opposing or slandering it. One who opposes the Lotus Sutra when it is preached will still form a relationship with it by virtue of opposition, and will thereby attain Buddhahood eventually. A "poison drum" is a mythical drum daubed with poison; this is a reference to a statement in the Nirvana Sutra that once the poison drum is beaten, all those who hear it will die, even if they are not of the mind to listen to it. Similarly, when the correct teaching is preached, both those who embrace it and those who oppose it will equally receive the seeds of Buddhahood, and even those who oppose it will attain Buddhahood eventually. In this analogy, the "death" that results from hearing the correct teaching is the death of illusion or earthly desires.

purification of the six sense organs—"Benefits of the Teacher of the Law," the Lotus Sutra's nineteenth chapter, describes the benefits that accrue to those who seek and teach the Law in terms of the six senses. When our senses are purified, we can use all our faculties to understand things correctly, as they truly are, and thus can help others all the more.

Sado Exile—Government authorities, in collusion with corrupt Buddhist priests, planned but failed to execute Nichiren in September 1271. They then exiled him to Sado Island, a fate tantamount to a death sentence. But after more than two years, after he had won many new supporters there and when his predictions of internal revolt and foreign invasion came true, the government pardoned him.

seven kinds of treasures—Also, seven treasures or seven kinds of gems. Precious substances mentioned in the sutras. The list differs among the Buddhist scriptures. According to the Lotus Sutra, the seven are gold, silver, lapis lazuli, seashell, agate, pearl, and carnelian (LSOC, 209). Nichiren associates the seven kinds of treasures with the seven elements of practice: hearing the correct teaching, believing it, keeping the precepts, engaging in meditation, practicing assiduously, renouncing one's attachments, and reflecting on oneself (see WND-1, 299).

Shakyamuni—Also known as Gautama Buddha. The founder of Buddhism. This name comes from the clan to which his family belonged, the Shakya clan, and means "sage of Shakyas."

Soka Renaissance—In a notice dated November 28, 1991, Nichiren Shoshu excommunicated the Soka Gakkai, and that date has since then been considered our Spiritual Independence Day. The day marked a fresh start in the organization's efforts for worldwide kosen-rufu.

three existences—Past existence, present existence, and future existence. Used to indicate all of time, from the eternal past, through the present, into the eternal future. In Buddhism, they are the three aspects of the eternity of life, linked inseparably by the law of cause and effect.

three obstacles and four devils—Various obstacles and hindrances to the practice of Buddhism. Nichiren cites a commentary that reads, "As practice progresses and understanding grows, the three obstacles and four devils emerge in confusing form, vying with one another to interfere. . . . One should be neither influenced nor frightened by them."

three powerful enemies—Three types of arrogant people who persecute those who propagate the Lotus Sutra in the evil age after Shakyamuni's death: arrogant lay people, arrogant priests, and arrogant false sages.

Thus Come One—One of the ten honorable titles of a Buddha, meaning one who has come from the realm of truth. It indicates that a Buddha embodies the fundamental truth of all phenomena and has grasped the law of causality spanning past, present, and future.

treasure tower—A tower adorned with jewels and treasures, the most famous of which appears in the Lotus Sutra. It is described as massive, thousands of miles high. Nichiren viewed the tower as an allegory for human life in its enlightened state achieved through chanting Nam-myoho-renge-kyo.